SCORPIO

SCORPIO

24 October–22 November

PATTY GREENALL & CAT JAVOR

MQP

Published by MQ Publications Limited
12 The Ivories
6–8 Northampton Street
London N1 2HY
Tel: 020 7359 2244
Fax: 020 7359 1616
Email: mail@mqpublications.com
Website: www.mqpublications.com

Illustrations: Gerry Baptist

ISBN: 1-84072-655-5

1 3 5 7 9 0 8 6 4 2

Printed in Italy

WHAT IS ASTROLOGY?

Astrology is the practice of interpreting the positions and movements of celestial bodies with regard to what they can tell us about life on Earth. In particular it is the study of the cycles of the Sun, Moon, and the planets of our solar system, and their journeys through the twelve signs of the zodiac—Aries, Taurus, Gemini, Cancer, Leo, Virgo, Libra, Scorpio, Sagittarius, Capricorn, Aquarius, and Pisces—all of which provide astrologers with a rich diversity of symbolic information and meaning.

Astrology has been labeled a science, an occult magical practice, a religion, and an art, yet it cannot be confined by any one of these descriptions. Perhaps the best way to describe it is as an evolving tradition.

Throughout the world, for as far back as history can inform us, people have been looking up at the skies and attaching stories and meanings to what they see there. Neolithic peoples in Europe built huge stone structures such as Stonehenge in southern England in order to plot the cycles of the Sun and Moon, cycles that were so important to a fledgling agricultural society. There are star-lore traditions in the ancient cultures of India, China, South America, and Africa, and among the indigenous people of Australia. The ancient Egyptians plotted the rising of the star Sirius, which marked the annual flooding of the Nile, and in ancient Babylon, astronomer-priests would perform astral divination in the service of their king and country.

Since its early beginnings, astrology has grown, changed, and diversified into a huge body of knowledge that has been added to by many learned men and women throughout history. It has continued to evolve and become richer and more informative, despite periods when it went out of favor because of religious, scientific, and political beliefs.

Offering us a deeper knowledge of ourselves, a profound insight into what motivates, inspires, and, in some cases, hinders, our ability to be truly our authentic selves, astrology equips us better to make the choices and decisions that confront us daily. It is a wonderful tool, which can be applied to daily life and our understanding of the world around us.

The horoscope—or birth chart—is the primary tool of the astrologer and the position of the Sun, Moon, Mercury, Venus, Mars, Jupiter, Saturn,

Uranus, Neptune, and Pluto at the moment a person was born are all considered when one is drawn up. Each planet has its own domain, affinities, and energetic signature, and the aspects or relationships they form to each other when plotted on the horoscope reveal a fascinating array of information. The birth, or Sun, sign is the sign of the zodiac that the Sun was passing through at the time of birth. The energetic signature of the Sun is concerned with a person's sense of uniqueness and self-esteem. To be a vital and creative individual is a fundamental need, and a person's Sun sign represents how that need most happily manifests in that person. This is one of the most important factors taken into account by astrologers. Each of the twelve Sun signs has a myriad of ways in which it can express its core meaning. The more a person learns about their individual Sun sign, the more they can express their own unique identity.

ZODIAC WHEEL

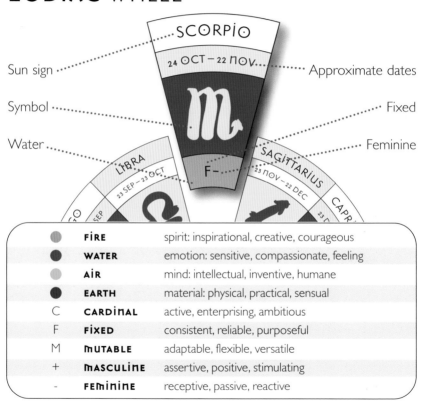

Sun sign

Symbol

Water

SCORPIO

24 OCT – 22 NOV.

♏

F–

Approximate dates

Fixed

Feminine

LIBRA
23 SEP – 23 OCT

SAGITTARIUS
23 NOV – 22 DEC

CAPR

🔴	**FIRE**	spirit: inspirational, creative, courageous
⚫	**WATER**	emotion: sensitive, compassionate, feeling
⚪	**AIR**	mind: intellectual, inventive, humane
⚫	**EARTH**	material: physical, practical, sensual
C	**CARDINAL**	active, enterprising, ambitious
F	**FIXED**	consistent, reliable, purposeful
M	**MUTABLE**	adaptable, flexible, versatile
+	**MASCULINE**	assertive, positive, stimulating
-	**FEMININE**	receptive, passive, reactive

PART ONE

THE **ESSENTIAL** SCORPIO

RULERSHİPS

Scorpio is the eighth sign of the zodiac, is one of the Water signs, and is traditionally ruled by the planet Mars, although the transformational energy of the planet Pluto has an affinity with Scorpio too. Its symbol is the Scorpion, but some prefer the symbolism of the Snake or the Eagle when referring to this sign. Scorpio is a Fixed and Feminine sign. There are earthly correspondences of everything in life for each of the Sun signs. The part of the human body that Scorpio represents is the genitals. Gemstones for Scorpio are yellow topaz, jasper, pyrope garnet, and obsidian. Scorpio also signifies blackthorn trees, heather, vineyards and orchards, eagles and reptiles, as well as muddy ground, lava, and cemeteries. It is also associated with butchers, psychiatrists, morticians, embalming, reincarnation, and the cycle of death and rebirth.

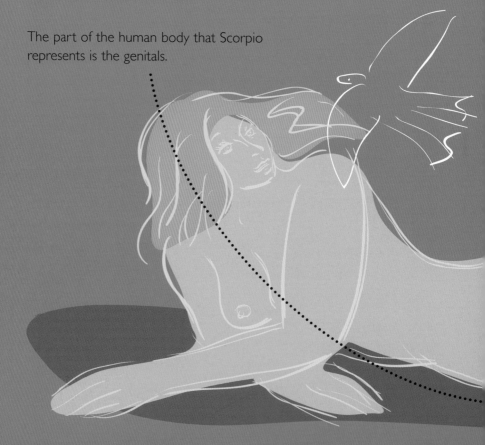

SCORPIO

The part of the human body that Scorpio represents is the genitals.

PERSO⊙⊓ALITY

"Passionate" is a word that's often used to describe Scorpio, and it's likely to be the reason why Scorpio enjoys a reputation for sexual prowess. A strongly sensual disposition is certainly one facet of their character but passion embodies their entire approach to life. Scorpios are creative, determined, and intensely insatiable people who aren't afraid to go "all the way." They'll give their all to a cause, so in bed, for example, they'll go deep into the dark, mysterious unknown, totally losing themselves in their sexual feelings and emerging refreshed and alive. But it would be the same for any activity that they indulge in; they don't go in for half-measures—it's all or nothing with them.

Another aspect of Scorpio lies in the sign's theme of death and rebirth. Some might find this scary, but not Scorpio. Scorpios understand the need for things that are past their expiration date to decline and die; that way they become the fertilizer for creative regeneration and with it a new, improved expression of life. Scorpios waste nothing; as far as they're concerned, everything can be reused, remade, and reborn, and this is a cycle through which they experience almost everything in life.

Their ability to go "all the way" means that Scorpios are often very successful. However, it's never really obvious to anyone but themselves what they're actually about. They are subtle, secretive beings, who are innately aware of what other people can do with sensitive information, so they protect themselves and the things that matter to them by controlling their tongues and giving very little away. Indeed, they possess an almost rigid self-control. They also project a slightly dangerous image of immense power and quiet command that helps prevent them from exposing even the slightest degree of vulnerability. It would be unfair, however, to surmise that Scorpios are cold, hard characters. They *can* be like that, particularly if they perceive some sort of a threat, but they also have deep, hypersensitive feelings.

They aren't exactly charitable people and aren't in the habit of supporting the underdog unless it's simply out of admiration for the effort that the underdog is putting in, or unless they have something to gain from it themselves. For they do respect and admire others for their achievements, strength of character, and determination, but Scorpio's regard must be earned; it's not given without good reason. Not surprisingly, Scorpios react well to competition and, in fact, have a quietly competitive streak. They expect other people to try to beat them at their game. On the rare occasions when they lose out, they'll remember it forever and will endeavor to improve their own personal performance. That's their way of righting a wrong, but it won't stop them from holding the winner in high esteem. Indeed, they'll be the first to congratulate anyone who outdoes them, yet often they'll be seething inside and vowing to get their own back!

Competition in what they see as their personal territory, particularly in the areas of career and intimate relationships, is another matter altogether. Nobody is ever allowed to encroach on these aspects of their life; Scorpios are always on their guard against people who try to take away the things that they've invested their heart and soul in. They'll see off any competition by going straight for someone's weaknesses, and they'll do so with pinpoint accuracy. Even if someone doesn't have any obvious weak spot, Scorpios will create one and a fight to the death may well ensue. Some say that you have to watch your back with a Scorpio, but it would be more accurate to say that you should never think you can pull a fast one on them. They have a penetrating insight that sees straight through any confidence trick or hidden agenda and they refuse to be anyone's fool.

Most people are unaware of the incredible inner world and drive to succeed possessed by Scorpios, and they probably couldn't care less, unless they are directly affected by it. Then they'll bemoan the fact that Scorpio is so very controlling, but they're probably simply jealous that Scorpio gets in their way. Scorpios not only attract jealousy, but can also be very jealous people themselves. They don't like seeing others with things that they want but don't have; the positive side of this is that it inspires and motivates them to access their immense creativity and use it to achieve their desires.

Meeting Scorpios for the first time is always a slightly unnerving experience because of the intense way in which they turn their attention so fixedly upon you. On the one hand, that sort of undivided attention can be rather flattering and very compelling; it's easy to be drawn into Scorpio's intoxicating sphere. On the other hand, they aren't paying so much attention simply out of friendly interest. They know how to spot an opportunity like an eagle spots its prey on the ground from the mountaintop, so their heightened curiosity is likely to have some other purpose than what is immediately apparent on the surface. They have a built-in sonar system—some call it intuition—that makes them very perceptive when it comes to other people. They like to uncover the secrets and mysteries that lie hidden in the dark recesses of people's psyches and they want to enrich themselves with the knowledge and understanding that other individuals have gained from life's experiences. Yet it's not for purely selfish reasons that they're looking to make a deep and intimate connection; they're seeking a mutually beneficial bond.

And that is where the sweet, loving, and nurturing sensitivity of the Scorpio really comes into its own. What others may see as redundant or even unpleasant in their own personal makeup, Scorpio accepts, cherishes, and supports, remaking, molding, and manipulating it until it's reborn out of the darkness and brought into the light transformed into a virtue. This amazing ability to have a life-changing effect on the people around them is just one of the reasons why Scorpios inspire such powerful emotions and why they gain the devotion of the select few who are lucky enough to be taken into the deep, passionate embrace of the Scorpio heart.

CAREER & MONEY

In their working life, Scorpios are determined and dedicated. They know that hard work is what they need in order to acquire the power and status they desire. They're ambitious and usually have a higher end in sight than what is immediately apparent. Many Scorpios devote themselves to building a substantial career over a period of time, and although they wouldn't say no to a well-thought-out get-rich-quick scheme, they would be more likely to take the harder but more certain road to success; that would have more meaning for them. Scorpios have a powerful character, even when they're working in the most menial positions, so they usually get the attention and respect they deserve. They're not people who are easy to forget!

Their ability to reach above and beyond things means that they are excellent at seeing the potential in something and finding the best possible way to develop it. They sense people's hidden motivations, have a very finely tuned sixth sense and, if there's some mystery to be solved, will follow a lead with interest, enthusiasm, and a determination to get to the bottom of things.

Although Scorpios can work successfully in partnerships, they aren't so comfortable when there are many people to cooperate and liaise with. They are best working on their own or with just one other person, but they can be trusted to stay with whatever they are assigned to do.

Their talents are multifaceted and their drive so powerful that it's possible for them to succeed at almost anything they put their minds to, although, as transformation is their keyword, any career connected to improvement and change, particularly concerning the human psyche or the human body, will be excellent for Scorpios. Such careers include psychology, psychiatry, analysis, research, detective work, the army, surgery, healing, and preaching. Because there's a strong creative side to Scorpio, particularly in finding new uses for things that others may have discarded, Scorpios might also be happy working in furniture or art restoration, theater or film-set design, or as antique dealers.

When it comes to money, Scorpio's usual all-or-nothing stance is again apparent. Scorpios will spend money like water when they have it, but will hold back completely when they don't, and they know exactly when to hold back. They can be very generous, but they certainly won't be if they're in the company of a skinflint since they regard skinflints as fools and don't suffer fools gladly. Moreover, they're better at handling other people's money than their own; then their skill for seeing future trends and the potential in things can really prove useful.

THE SCORPIO **CHILD**

The penetrating stare of the Scorpio child is obvious almost from the moment he or she comes into the world. It's not a case of "the lights are on but nobody's home;" Scorpio babies focus their innocent attention on their immediate environment and take great interest in everything that's going on around them. They swing between being noisy when their demands aren't being met, to being silent but deeply contemplative watchers of the world.

As they grow older and start moving about, often clutching their favorite toy or security blanket, they become extremely cute and giggly. They form a very strong attachment to one or both parents, and they can either be lively and talkative or silent and snuggly with them. When learning a new skill in the playground or at school, Scorpio children are determined and patient. If they don't achieve success straight away, then they'll keep trying and if anyone, child or adult, thinks of interfering or of lending a hand, they'll only receive an angry, frustrated retort in return. If they can possibly help it, they won't let themselves be defeated by anyone or anything. They have wonderful imaginations and can be rather extrovert, but they tend to become more secretive about what they really think or feel as they get older. This is a form of self-protection that they develop because of their deep sensitivity; they don't want to expose themselves to the pain of insult or criticism.

Scorpio children are cautious in forming friendships. Even when they're part of a large group, they'll only be close with one or two friends as they're often wary of their powerful emotional reactions when things turn sour. They counter betrayal with vengeance, have long memories, and don't easily forgive. As they grow into adolescence, young Scorpios often get deeply involved in dissecting the dynamics of personal relationships and exploring the social concerns of the time, testing the strength of their attitudes and feelings as well as those of others. It's rarely a comfortable process for anyone, particularly the young Scorpios themselves but, with their sensitivity combined with their strength, and their seriousness combined with their stimulating qualities, they're very intriguing people to have around.

PERFECT **GiFTS**

Buying a present for someone who is so hard to read is a very difficult task. Many Scorpios would probably prefer a gift of money, or to be bought a meal or a drink instead of being given something that they don't want, for they are pretty particular about their likes and dislikes. The best gift anyone could give to a Scorpio is loyalty; that's something that they will treasure for a lifetime—as long as it's guaranteed to last that long.

However, if you are buying a gift, there are a few things to keep in mind. Scorpios like mysteries and enjoy trying to solve them, so books and games with a mystery theme or some underlying conundrum will keep their attention for hours. They also appreciate word games or any gift that will stretch their minds. They also love to have any kind of surveillance equipment, but be sure to give it discreetly! They wouldn't like others to know about it. But of course, they may own it already and you can never be sure of that, so give them the receipt, just in case, so they can exchange it if they want to. But, generally speaking, Scorpios don't really expect much in the way of gifts; a little kindness and thoughtfulness will go a long way with them.

FAVORiTE **FOODS**

Food is one of the sensual pleasures in life so it forms an important part of Scorpio's routine, but they are not usually overly preoccupied with it. If they're alone, Scorpios will often forget to eat; they prefer to view mealtimes as an opportunity to sit down and spend time with the people they share their life with. Breakfast is possibly the only meal that they won't mind eating alone for then they can read the daily paper or sort out their private thoughts before they get on with their day.

Scorpios have rather sophisticated taste buds and aren't afraid to try a new taste or combinations of flavors so long as they know what they're being served up in advance, for they like to have a certain amount of control over what they put in their mouths. They won't be satisfied with bland or boring food since they like strong flavors and expect what they're eating to taste of something. Their food doesn't have to be complicated, simply tasty. If you look in their pantry cupboards, you'll find that they're usually full of inventive gourmet condiments or unusual products that will add some bite to standard fare. When they dine out, they'll definitely have their favorite dishes and may well become very attached to certain dishes in certain restaurants—a superior steak tartare at one, for example, or the tasty grilled eggplant and couscous at another.

FASHIΟΠ & **STYLE**

When it comes to clothing, the Scorpio cliché is, of course, black leather from top to toe. There's something about the strength of leather, its sensual effect against the skin, and the power it conveys to others that appeals to the Scorpio sense of style. Even Scorpios who have never bought a pair of leather pants are sure to have a black leather belt or jacket hanging around.

Scorpios have three looks; commanding, mysterious, and sexy, and depending on their mood, they'll choose one or a combination of all three. They could dress to project a dangerous, controlling "don't mess with me, I'm in a sharp suit but my tongue is sharper" image. Alternatively, they might sport an ever-so-slightly hippie-ish look, softly yet suggestively hinting "I know secrets that will change your life forever, but are you sure you want to hear them?" Or, finally, they may go for the sexy "I'm only revealing flesh because I'm so hot, touch me if you dare, but don't blame me if you get burned" effect.

But whatever they wear, Scorpios are never fashion victims. They enjoy noting what's in style, but they have a talent for achieving an up-to-date look by remodeling the quality garments that they already own, or those that they find in vintage clothing stores. Their color of choice is black, but they look wonderful in any of the deeper shades of red, plum, or green. It's a rare Scorpio who goes in for pretty pastels or bright lollipop colors.

IDEAL HOMES

The Scorpio home may not look much from the outside and might even be somewhat plain. In fact, it can blend right into the environment so that it's actually rather difficult to find. That might be because it simply doesn't stand out or because it's camouflaged by trees and shrubs, in which case, like a cave, there will be many hidden treasures on the inside. It's usually a rather stylish place in a dark, mysterious kind of way—intriguing, and with unusual or enigmatic-looking ornaments, such as a head with staring eyes that might even be a genuine shrunken head picked up on Scorpio's travels!

Although Scorpios will welcome anyone who dares to enter, their homes aren't the kind of place where you'd simply drop by without an invitation or prior arrangement—they probably won't even open the door. But they'll have the best surveillance equipment that their money can buy. If they can afford it, then they'll opt for a video entry system that allows them to know who's outside before they even reach the door. They like to play safe and protect their secrets.

PART TWO

RISING SIGNS

WHAT IS A RISING SIGN?

Your rising sign is the zodiacal sign that could be seen rising on the eastern horizon at the time and place of your birth. Each sign takes about two and a half hours to rise—approximately one degree every four minutes. Because it is so fast moving, the rising sign represents a very personal part of the horoscope, so even if two people were born on the same day and year as one another, their different rising signs will make them very different people.

It is easier to understand the rising sign when the entire birth chart is seen as a circular map of the heavens. Imagine the rising sign—or ascendant—at the eastern point of the circle. Opposite is where the Sun sets—the descendant. The top of the chart is the part of the sky that is above, where the Sun reaches at midday, and the bottom of the chart is below, where the Sun would be at midnight. These four points divide the circle, or birth chart, into four. Those quadrants are then each divided into three, making a total of twelve, known as houses, each of which represents a certain aspect of life. Your rising sign corresponds to the first house and establishes which sign of the zodiac occupied each of the other eleven houses when you were born.

All of which makes people astrologically different from one another; not all Scorpios are alike! The rising sign generally indicates what a person looks like. For instance, people with Leo, the sign of kings, rising, probably walk with a noble air and find that people often treat them like royalty. Those that have Pisces rising frequently have soft and sensitive looks and they might find that people are forever pouring their hearts out to them.

The rising sign is a very important part of the entire birth chart and should be considered in combination with the Sun sign and all the other planets!

THE RISING SIGNS FOR SCORPIO

To work out your rising sign, you need to know your exact time of birth—if hospital records aren't available, try asking your family and friends. Now turn to the charts on pages 38–43. There are three charts, covering New York, Sydney, and London, all set to Greenwich Mean Time. Choose the correct chart for your place of birth and, if necessary, add or subtract the number of hours difference from GMT (for example, Sydney is approximately ten hours ahead, so you need to subtract ten hours from your time of birth). Then use a ruler to carefully find the point where your GMT time of birth meets your date of birth—this point indicates your rising sign.

SCORPIO WITH **ARIES** RISING

The planet Mars ruling both Scorpio and Aries results in very active and energetic people indeed. Highly intelligent self-starters, who brook no opposition when they are carrying their plans forward and fulfilling their ambitions, they attack life with a shrewd, no-nonsense approach. When they're feeling lighthearted, they'll be game for a good time. They're great with children and will be playful and demonstrative. But when it's time to get serious, they do so with the most profound intensity. They can tune into someone else's way of relating at the snap of a finger and can zero in on the core of a matter, cutting through any ambiguity and nonsense. With Aries rising, the naturally deep insight of Scorpio can no longer simply sit back, observe and feel its way through the complexities of life and other people's psyches; it must become actively involved, penetrating to the heart of each person and each situation, and uncovering their every hidden detail. At first glance, Scorpios with Aries rising appear to be open, enthusiastic, and uncomplicated, but that's only the surface; beneath lies a fathomless reservoir of thought and sensitivity.

SCORPiO WiTH **TAURUS** RiSiNG

Scorpios with Taurus rising appear relaxed, totally at ease, and sure of themselves. This attitude acts like a magnet that draws to their side those in need of a strong, calming influence. They handle flighty people with a solid sensitivity but if they're challenged, they deliver their rebuke as if they had an iron fist in a velvet glove. Deeply passionate and often very physically attractive, they can be hedonistic, yet still manage to keep their feet on the ground. They have good taste and usually like the finer things in life. They are powerful, elegant people who know their own mind and won't let it be changed easily, if at all. Their calm, stubborn patience allows them to sit out any disturbance in knowing, unruffled silence. They have an ability to attract material success and riches, often by working long and hard, but they know when to quit and will leave themselves plenty of time to unwind. They work well with others in a professional and personal capacity for they have a need to understand people, and themselves, through their dealings with others.

SCORPIO WITH **GEMINI** RISING

With Gemini rising Scorpio is given the gift of gab. These Scorpios can convey even the most complex thoughts and feelings with alacrity and eloquence. However, they are often rather shy and nervous in the company of strangers, letting only their nearest and dearest enjoy the benefit of their wise wit. Once they get going however, it's hard to stop them because they have something to say about everything. They are quick, deep thinkers, who display an intelligence that many would find hard to keep up with. With a deep sensitivity and desire to be of help to others, they choose their words carefully and reveal a deep understanding that often has a very healing effect on people. Nimble and dexterous, they often excel at physical activities that require self-control and discipline, such as fast-moving sports, gymnastics and ballet. Their sometimes uneasy disposition requires that they keep busy, either physically or mentally. They need a brisk walk, run, or workout for them to function smoothly. These multi-taskers can handle many chores at once while understanding what is required of them *and* keeping a conversation going.

SCORPIO WITH **CANCER** RISING

These are some of the most sweetly sensitive Scorpios. Although on the outside they appear extremely tough, protective of their own feelings, and untouchable, when Cancer is rising they're as tuned in to the emotional atmosphere around them as it's possible to be. They feel their way through life using their unusually keen instinct and sharp intuition. Although they have a good sense of humor and can be incredibly playful, they exude a sense of superiority and prefer the company of their exclusive circle of friends and family to opening up their social life to others. They are highly creative at work and at home, never at a loose end or at a loss for something to do. Give them a brush and they'll start painting. They enjoy renewing their surroundings and making their home a more comfortable place. They have amazingly retentive memories and sometimes have a habit of clinging to the past, but they can make the most of both of these characteristics, either by working in restoration or antiques, by teaching, or by choosing any area of work that involves bringing the past into the present.

SCORPIO WITH **LEO** RISING

There is a seam of very clever and rich creativity lying deep in the heart of the Scorpio with Leo rising. These people have a powerful desire to explore their talents and put their many skills on show. They're strongly influenced by family and background, even though they spend much of their early life carving out their own path and expressing themselves as individuals. Highly expressive and possessing a creative flair, they are also fearless and courageous and have no problem tackling single-handed even the most daunting forms of artistry. They often appear quiet, serene, and supremely confident, as well as totally oblivious to the mundane trifles that other people spend their time worrying about, but their sharp minds miss nothing and their intuitive sense makes them aware of the emotional undercurrents in any situation in which they find themselves. Fiercely passionate and territorial, there is a strong jealous streak running through them that surfaces whenever others attempt to usurp their position. When pushed, they have a hot, fiery temper but that can die down just as quickly as it flares up. Underneath it all, they are generous, but they forget nothing.

SCORPIO WITH **VIRGO** RISING

Just because the Scorpio with Virgo rising appears modest and unassuming, it would be ridiculous to assume that these people are any less intense or powerful than any other Scorpios. The keen, analytical persona that lies behind that quiet, aloof, self-contained exterior almost fanatically sifts through every bit of information gathered by any of its senses. These Scorpios file everything away in their vast memory and can call it up in an instant. They have a voracious appetite for learning, particularly through the quiet, contemplative practice of reading. But they also enjoy conversation, during which they often seem to be grilling the person they are speaking to by asking endless probing questions. They have brilliant minds and can sort and analyze information in a flash. Although they never really start an argument, they seem to attract lively repartee. They are reliable and friendly—the kind of people who help to make the world go round quickly and more efficiently.

SCORPIO WITH **LIBRA** RISING

Scorpios with Libra rising are very personable and attractive. They often have impeccable, old-fashioned manners and are polite and reserved, but they always have a smile on their faces. Diplomatic and eloquent, they have a way of making a point without upsetting anyone. Lovers of beauty, luxury and the good things in life, their interest is aroused by both sensual and esthetic forms of pleasure, which gives them a powerful desire to surround themselves with sumptuous, elegant, and expensive possessions. Their homes will be rich, inviting, and visually stunning and will be decorated in the height of good taste. But while they have a propensity for making money (the accumulation of wealth helps to provide them with a sense of material security), they gain their real self-confidence through the forging of and deep involvement in intimate, personal relationships. These Scorpios are perhaps among the softer, sweeter ones. They are innately cheerful even in the most extreme circumstances. They are also good-looking, refined, and penetrating, yet they are true survivors, who manage to combine wry humor with an optimistic outlook on life.

SCORPIO WITH **SCORPIO** RISING

♏ The double Scorpios are truly impressive individuals. They are so aware of their environment that they seem to have eyes in the back of their heads! Determined, self-reliant, and willful, they approach life with energetic enthusiasm but are cautious enough not to leap before they have had a very good look. They deliberately maintain an aura of mystery, giving very little away about their plans, instead preferring to achieve first and let everyone discuss it later. Despite their need to make strong and lasting connections, they're inclined, at first, to be suspicious of others, for they are always on the lookout for anyone who may be trying to get the better of them; they definitely won't be taken advantage of. They have a keen sense of intuition, but that doesn't always mean that their suspicions are correct. On the other hand, their insight and cleverness enable them to help other people to see their own talents and fulfill their potential. When it comes to work, double Scorpios are doubly good at handling money, but they also make life-changing therapists and leaders in the world of psychology.

SCORPIO WITH **SAGITTARIUS** RISING

♐ These are some of the most gregarious of the Scorpio clan. They are more spontaneous and less self-controlled than the others, at least on the surface. With Sagittarius rising, they have a more philosophical and inclusive approach to life rather than the inward, exclusive approach of other

Scorpios. With their tendency to immerse themselves in matters strange and elusive, they possess keen skills of detection and a talent for the rooting out of mysteries. They feel their way intuitively until they pluck, as if from nowhere, the answers they were searching for. For these Scorpios, finding answers and discovering as much as they can about the undercurrents that drive the world is a strong motivating force. They readily open themselves up to new ideas, experiences, and opportunities for the specific purpose of gaining a deeper understanding of and connection with all aspects of life. However, it's not always easy for them to keep up their high-spirited front. These Scorpios need time alone. They would appreciate the healing daily ritual of time spent in solo contemplation; it would help them to restore their energy levels when they feel drained from absorbing too much from the outside world.

SCORPIO WITH **CAPRICORN** RISING

It may appear that Scorpios with Capricorn rising are the cool, strong, silent type, immensely self-controlled and staunch supporters of tradition, rules, and regulations, but there's just enough of the anarchist in them to stop them from becoming an anachronism. They have an original yet practical mind that never ceases to provide them with solutions to the problems that they face during their ambitious and determined rise to the top. They make friends easily and are quick to associate with the right people. Building a better future is what concerns them most, but it's not just for themselves, it's for everyone. Their aim is to make the world a better place but, of course, they'll enjoy some of the benefits, too! These Scorpios have an interesting and admirable humanitarian streak, which is part of the reason why they like to join organizations that support their interests. Steady and sure-footed, they pace themselves and are rarely found making a wrong move or doing anything that they might regret. And although they take their time as they steadily unravel concepts and ideas, each step leads them closer toward deeper understanding.

SCORPIO WITH **AQUARIUS** RISING

The Scorpio with Aquarius rising is intelligent, reasonable, and just a teeny bit eccentric, although no one would realize it because they appear to be the picture of quiet dignity and thoughtful strength. What people do notice is their good looks and gentle demeanor. Friendly yet aloof, humane yet unsentimental, these individuals have an inventive, questing mind that rejects nothing, no matter how off-the-wall, until they have picked it apart from every perspective imaginable. They can be extremely stubborn and dogmatic in their opinions, but since they've spent so much of their time building those opinions on strong foundations, it's hardly surprising. With such a vast store of abilities and talents to draw on, Scorpios with Aquarius rising often reach the very top of whatever profession they choose; they simply seem to shine. They have a knack for seeing opportunities and for being in the right place at the right time, and if there's ever a promotion going at work, they'll be considered for it early on. Even-tempered, unassuming yet very able and well-presented, this Scorpio makes a great friend, confidante and, especially, boss. They have the perfect blend of detachment and sensitivity, as well as a great way with people.

SCORPIO WITH **PISCES** RISING

With eyes that seem focused intently beyond the physical world, the Scorpio with Pisces rising is an imaginative and inspiring soul on a quest to discover thoughts and feelings that have never been thought and felt before. Whether this takes these Scorpios on a magical journey into the heart and mind, or to faraway lands for a unique experience of another culture or religion, they will always push back the boundaries and go where others wouldn't dare dream of going. They are unique individuals, who enjoy being on their own. This gives them a chance to recharge their batteries or to delve into their imaginations and so create a new reality for the world to experience. They aren't particularly ambitious but they are high achievers in a mystical, mysterious kind of way. Highly intuitive and switched-on, the intensity of their passion is not immediately apparent as they seem "not quite there," but passion is a driving force with them and it makes them as tenacious and determined as other Scorpios. These are very emotional, idealistic people, often shy but with huge reserves of compassion and sympathy. A Scorpio with Pisces rising is like a spiritual guru, embracing and teaching anyone who is willing to delve deep into their own psyche.

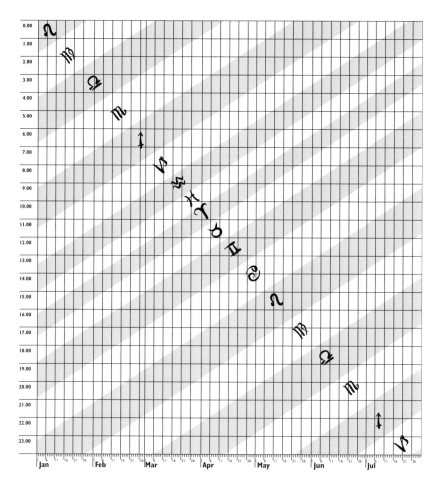

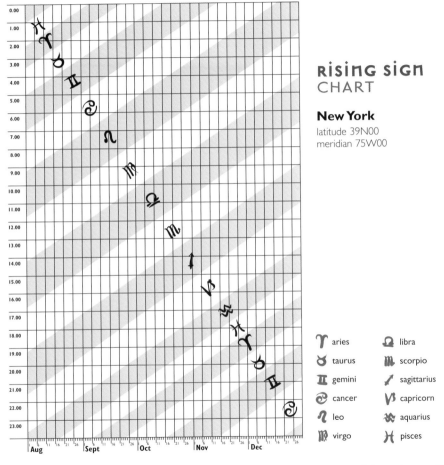

RISING SIGN
CHART

New York

latitude 39N00
meridian 75W00

♈	aries	♎	libra
♉	taurus	♏	scorpio
♊	gemini	♐	sagittarius
♋	cancer	♑	capricorn
♌	leo	♒	aquarius
♍	virgo	♓	pisces

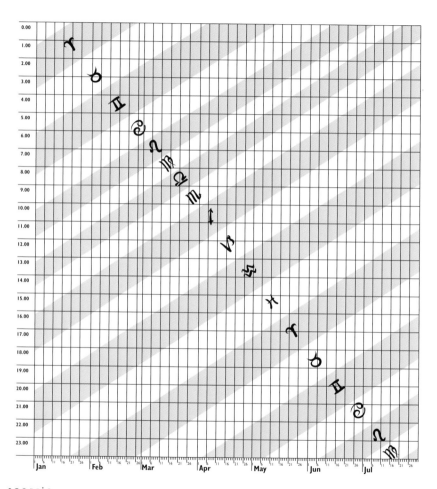

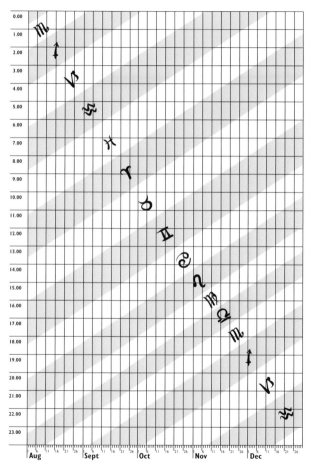

RISING SIGN
CHART

Sydney

latitude 34S00
meridian 150E00

♈	aries	♎	libra
♉	taurus	♏	scorpio
♊	gemini	♐	sagittarius
♋	cancer	♑	capricorn
♌	leo	♒	aquarius
♍	virgo	♓	pisces

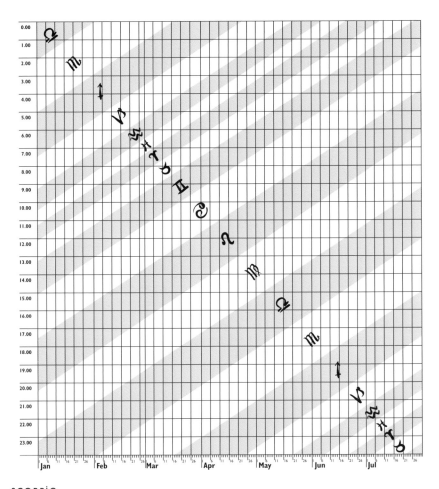

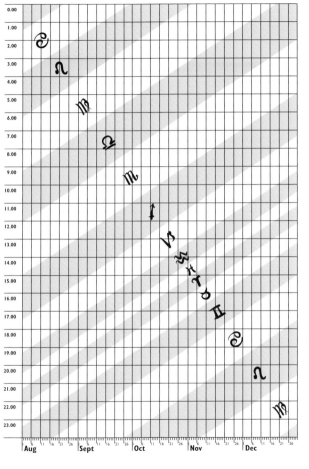

RiSiNG SiGN
CHART

London

latitude 51N30
meridian 0W00

♈ aries	♎ libra
♉ taurus	♏ scorpio
♊ gemini	♐ sagittarius
♋ cancer	♑ capricorn
♌ leo	♒ aquarius
♍ virgo	♓ pisces

PART THREE

RELATIONSHIPS

THE SCORPIO **FRIEND**

Scorpios are wary of making new friends until they've had a chance to dissect the potential friend's character. It's not that they're impolite or standoffish; they generally smile kindly, make a few gentle inquiries then sit back, offering an unspoken invitation for the other person to reveal as much or as little as they would like to about themselves. Too much, and Scorpio will get bored, thinking, perhaps, that this person is all talk and no action. Too little, and Scorpio might sense that the person is hiding something, and then they'll dig for more information. What Scorpios are looking for is something in the middle—a person who is intelligent yet entertaining, compassionate yet confident. They don't mind people with strong opinions or sensitive feelings as long as there is some depth to them. After long, searching periods of exposure to a new person, Scorpios become more relaxed and trusting, and will, little by little, proffer more information about themselves.

The longer someone has been able to call a Scorpio "friend," the longer they'll have had a stalwart ally at their side. However, because Scorpios possess a powerful need for self-protection, they rarely drop their guard completely. If they ever experience betrayal, then heaven help the person responsible. Scorpio's retaliation will be stinging and painfully permanent, unless of course that now ex-friend is prepared to do a lot of groveling.

SCORPIO WITH **ARIES**

♈ Scorpio and Aries can work very well together when they have an objective in mind. Aries likes a mission and Scorpio always has an agenda, so as a team, they are formidable and unconquerable. Both have unstoppable energy and a passionate drive, however, if they're left to drift without an aim, their friendship could prove to be less than compatible because they're fundamentally very different. Aries is all about action, impulsiveness, and spontaneity where Scorpio is all about deep thought, deliberation, and intensity. In small doses, anyone can tolerate anyone, however, this pairing is more repelling than compelling.

SCORPIO WITH **TAURUS**

♉ Scorpio has deep affection and respect for Taurus, while Taurus will be patient and understanding, even when Scorpio is in one of the sign's darker moods. These two signs are opposite one another in the zodiac, which means that there are similarities between them. For example, both can be very stubborn so stand-offs and power struggles could be the result. Taurus is very down-to-earth but will be fascinated by Scorpio, who goes much deeper than that. They'll either be so taken with one another that they can't imagine life without the other, or so repulsed that they can't imagine life with the other. But the solution will soon become apparent and they won't have a problem agreeing on it.

SCORPIO WITH GEMINI

This is an odd couple for friendship. Scorpio is all depth, intensity, and brooding, while Gemini is light and airy and unable—or perhaps unwilling because that would require attention and focus—to reach the same profundity. It would be difficult for these two Sun signs to see eye to eye but, on the other hand, certain planetary influences in their charts could actually make this into a truly productive pairing. Where Gemini has the ideas, Scorpio can see the big picture. Together they could make a storm in a teacup. There is potential here for amazing things.

SCORPIO WITH CANCER

Cancer and Scorpio friends make a pretty perceptive duo. With just the two of them together, they could probably spend all day discussing what lies behind so and so's antics—and they'd probably have it spot on. There's so much of interest to find out. Both are into talking about people's feelings and motivations and if their gossip sessions turn a trifle bitchy, well, nobody else is listening so nobody ever gets hurt—and at least it provides them with a few giggles. When these two are out with a group of people, they share an unspoken feeling of support and understanding.

SCORPiO WiTH **LEO**

Since both have strong opinions, there could be a touch of resistance or tension in this friendship, which is fine so long as they're in agreement. When they are, they make a formidable team. They'll be attracted to one another because each senses something very promising in the other and, in the early stages, they'll find they have much in common, developing a compelling sense of rapport. However, while they respect and admire one another's strength of character, there will inevitably be moments when their opinions don't converge and then it could get rather loud and painful for them both—perhaps too hot to handle!

SCORPiO WiTH **ViRGO**

On the surface, these two seem so very different; Scorpio has a deep, emotional approach to life and Virgo has a subtle, physical one. And yet they share some similarities which they instinctively recognize in each other and which make it easy for a friendship to blossom. They both have a way of affirming the other's worth through their natural acceptance of and agreement with the other. Both are, to some extent, detectives, the one discovering the emotional side of things and the other the physical, so what they learn separately then feeds the other's desire for greater understanding. They may eventually come to rely on each other simply for emotional support; this will ensure a special kind of connection between them.

SCORPIO WITH **LIBRA**

If there were ever two friends who could share some secret verbal exchange to the exclusion of all others, then it's Libra and Scorpio. In a room full of people, you'll find these two sitting in a corner, chatting away, and exploring a whole host of intensely intellectual ideas. They'll be so totally absorbed in picking the other's point of view apart that they won't even notice that there might be a whole herd of other people who would love to join in their conversation. This pair make great friends but they'll need to do their best to include others, or else they'll be accused of cliquishness.

SCORPIO WITH **SCORPIO**

It may take a third person to bring these two together, just to break the ice, but once they get talking there will be a natural rapport between them. Two Scorpios will find many topics on which they're in complete agreement and they'll enjoy probing certain ideas and concepts in order to uncover connections that non-Scorpios would simply skim over. But if their opinions ever differ wildly and discussions turn into debates and debates into fights, then the fights will get personal and there'll be lots of hissing. However, both their lives will be enhanced by knowing one another. Each can provide the other with a heap of hugely interesting information to ponder over.

SCORPIO WITH **SAGITTARIUS**

This is a revealing and enlightening friendship and, like a good thriller, one that's hard to put down. Conversations between Scorpio and Sagittarius go deep and have a mind-expanding effect. Both have a way of getting the other interested and intrigued. However, while exploration of ideas and experience is their baseline, both have very different ways of approaching it. Sagittarius wants to head out on the town for spontaneous fun and action, while Scorpio would prefer holing up in the quiet corner of an interesting bar or bistro and observing the action at the same time as giving a wry running commentary on it.

SCORPIO WITH **CAPRICORN**

These two make firm friends. They not only have a lot to say to each other, but they're honestly intrigued by and respond to the other's take on things. While they respect each other's personal boundaries, it's still possible for both of them to feel very relaxed and comfortable in each other's company. They don't feel any pressure to put on a performance because they agree about many things, such as what to do, where to go, or what to talk about. They simply meld and get along as if they were always meant to be together.

SCORPIO WITH **AQUARIUS**

〰〰 When Scorpio and Aquarius have lots of interests in common, they'll enjoy spending time in each other's company because both will respect the other's commitment and depth of understanding. Aloof but friendly, the Aquarius reluctance to get personal will suit Scorpio well, because Scorpios prefer to reveal their inner sensitivity only to their loved ones. However, if there's even the smallest note of disagreement between them, then they'll steer well clear of one another because both can be stubborn and there's a feeling between them that something nasty might erupt. In social situations they should find it easy to maintain a comfortable level of banter, as long as it's in short bursts.

SCORPIO WITH **PISCES**

Scorpio and Pisces really connect, and because they feel a natural rapport they're able to let their hair down and have some seriously amusing, creative fun together. Scorpio is secretive and Pisces elusive, yet their sympathy for and sensitivity to each other are such that they share an exclusivity that's a complete mystery to everyone around them. Even if they don't see each other for months, or even years, they'll quickly get reacquainted when they meet again and will get on together as if they had never spent any time apart. They'll have an easy liking for one another, but their friendship is likely to go deeper than that.

THE **SCORPIO WOMAN** IN LOVE

Falling in love for the Scorpio woman is full of torments and pitfalls, not only for herself but for the lover who's courting her, so she's very cautious when it comes to getting up close and personal. And she does get up very close and very personal; superficial romantic liaisons aren't her style at all. This woman will constantly be testing the depth of commitment in the relationship, checking whether the level of passion is strong enough to sustain her interest, probing her partner's intellectual fortitude for inconsistencies, and seeking out any signs of hypocrisy. She has a basically suspicious nature when it comes to other people, most particularly her mate, because she knows that nobody is perfect and that everyone has a shadow side. She's certainly explored the dark corners of her own psyche with a ruthless attention to detail, so she isn't shy when it comes to foraging about in her man's.

The Scorpio woman expects to find faults and if she doesn't, then she's not doing her job properly. But faults don't worry her; she simply wants to be aware of the possible danger areas, then she'll dig, prod, and pick at them to find out whether they'll ever affect her sensitive heart and the longevity of the relationship. She's hypersensitive to the pain that can be caused by exposing herself to a careless, unfaithful, or untrustworthy partner, so even once her heart is engaged, she'll continue with the probing, but will offer in return loyalty, passion, and an all-encompassing love that is intoxicating in its intensity. She'll build an exclusive, secret world where she and her man can explore and love each other, unaffected by the goings-on and opinions of others. The rest of the world can go to the devil: she and her lover will be in heaven. It may be a slightly uncomfortable heaven, but for them it will be heaven nonetheless.

She's very possessive and jealous, and won't take kindly to any outsider meddling in their relationship or attempting to entice her lover away. Her watchful eyes are always on the lookout for other women flirting with her man. Even if they're just having a bit of lighthearted fun, she'll make one or both of them pay dearly with her stingingly painful response. She'll soon see off any competition and will make sure that her man will never even dream of betraying her again. She needs to be in control in order to feel secure and isn't averse to a little emotional blackmail so, since she's very skilled at eliciting a passionate response, she may even do some flirting herself to arouse her partner's sexual jealousy. If his reaction isn't powerful enough, she may even take things a step further. She's not afraid of a fight; in fact, she enjoys one because it will show her if her lover has enough substance and strength of character. A weak, wishy-washy man would be beneath contempt. This sensitive, sensual, sexy woman is a handful and she's certainly not for the fainthearted, but she's a fair lady who's worth winning.

SCORPIO WOMAN WITH **ARIES MAN**

 In love: With two such powerfully willful people it's very easy to see why this is such a volatile relationship. Tempers flare, passions rise, and the way the Scorpio woman and Aries man affect each other is positively explosive! For them it's like living on a knife edge suspended over a raging sea. She will love his strong sense of self, his confidence, and his go-get-'em attitude to life, just as he will adore her seductive femininity and admire the way she keeps her powerful emotions under strict control. There's definitely a pull between them and they can certainly feel it! They are both passionate and energetic, but in very different ways. She is a more serious, intense, and brooding type, and she will not tolerate infantile behavior, even when it is accompanied by the sort of cheery innocence Aries is prone to. If her anger rains down on his head, he'll flare up and raise the temperature to boiling point. The trouble is that when the matter has died down, he'll be happy to forgive and forget, but the super-sensitive Scorpio woman will remember every jibe and insult, and if she hasn't made him pay for it this time, he can be sure that she'll find a way to extract every last penance in the future. In the end, although this relationship can be exciting, it could all get a bit too much for both of them and her desire to get right to the bottom of this man could be thwarted by his warrior-like resistance.

In bed: Put your seatbelt on and get ready for the ride of a lifetime! There's an excitingly erotic and dangerous charge to the sexual relationship of the Scorpio woman and Aries man. Hot, heavy, steamy passion, is the only way to describe what happens when these two get between the sheets. They wanted sex? Well, they got it! But if this keeps going, they'll probably burn each other out. It's certainly one way to meet the challenge of a Scorpio/Aries relationship. The problem is that she has a need to achieve a deeper sexual intimacy than she's likely to get from the Ram man, who doesn't have the patience or the inclination for being deep and meaningful on every level all of the time. For both the Aries man and the Scorpio woman, this is one combination that must be tried just once. It's too good to miss! Their combined energy output is sure to take both of these Mars-ruled signs right up to their personal limits. But be warned: the intensity of the fire between them is tangible and both could end up sore in the most unexpected of places. Muscles they never knew they had will suddenly be put to good use. They'll have a mind-blowing experience that's sure to leave them both very different from before they met.

SCORPiO WOMAN WiTH **TAURUS MAN**

In love: Being opposites in the zodiac, the Scorpio woman and her Taurus man are like the Yin-Yang symbol, each half containing a minute essence of the other while also perfectly reflecting the whole. They seem familiar, even directly after meeting, because it's something they recognize in one another. It's a partnership that just feels right, like a hand in a well-fitting glove. They cling together in the sure knowledge that they complement and complete one another. With a Taurus man by her side, the Scorpio woman can feel the safety and security that are so important to her, while he can revel in the deep well of emotional devotion that she will keep in reserve only for him. From the moment they meet, they feel a mutual desire to indulge themselves in the finer things in life—there is a hedonistic quality to the relationship that makes no apology for the passionate pursuit of love, affection, and rich pleasure. However, the Taurus man is very possessive, while the Scorpio lady can become viciously jealous. As long as they stick to one another, these qualities can work perfectly together, but if one of them comes unstuck, there will be an almighty battle of wills. And as they are both incredibly stubborn, there could be harsh words followed by long spells of silence. But with understanding and mutual respect, this partnership will stand on very firm foundations and has the promise of getting better and better.

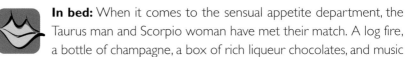 **In bed:** When it comes to the sensual appetite department, the Taurus man and Scorpio woman have met their match. A log fire, a bottle of champagne, a box of rich liqueur chocolates, and music playing gently in the background… They'll probably fall asleep some time before dawn, only to wake when the sun has risen, and gently but intensely make love all over again. It's not everyone who can fulfill the sexually savvy Scorpio woman's appetite for erotic pleasure, but she loves it when her man

gets down and dirty, and this one seems to have it all going for him. He is one hundred percent male and as solid and steady as a rock. His animalistic moves bring out the beast in her, yet he can also be controlled and measured and he has the stamina to stay with her as she cries out with delight—it's her way of showing true intimacy. For him, her mysterious femininity and liquid touch have an ecstatic quality that quenches his thirst for physical union and will have him drowning in the depths of her loving body. He wants to taste and savor every bit of her, while she could devour him whole. They are both such hungry lovers, it's difficult to tell who will eat up whom. But one thing is certain: they will never get bored with one another. For better or for worse, every entanglement will have a sexual overtone.

SCORPiO WOMAN WiTH **GEMiNi MAN**

 In love: There may be an initial attraction when Gemini man meets Scorpio woman. He certainly does have some very engaging qualities and appreciates her obvious sexuality. It is also possible that because they see things from such a different perspective, they may be able to give each other a whole new way of looking at life. But, fundamentally, they are as different as chalk and cheese. If they ever agree on anything it will be a miracle! She'll find it very hard work creating the depth of intimacy she's after with him, and he may find her possessiveness and intensity a little too restricting. Ms. Scorpio wants to be totally sure that the bond between them is unbreakable, but that only makes Mr. Gemini behave even more erratically and he may turn and fly, which is exactly the opposite of what she wants. Is it any wonder that they end up viewing each other with a certain amount of suspicion? In most cases, then, this isn't likely to be a long and happy union, unless, of course, other factors in their horoscopes indicate a strong compatibility. For example, he might be one of those unusual Gemini men who are more trousers than talk, and she could be one of those very rare Scorpio ladies who will allow her man a long leash. On the surface there isn't much to recommend the relationship for either of them, but look beyond that and there might just be some miraculous tie that ends up holding them together.

In bed: The Scorpio woman is unlikely to want more from the Gemini man than a one-night stand, and vice versa. It'll be fun while it lasts, and will give them both a good temporary fix, but after that, the only thing that might keep them attracted is those devilishly tempting one-night stands. Neither party could ever turn one down. She's a very sexy girl with a powerful desire to lure a man into a fathomless pit of passion, but he's usually just too lightweight for her. However, his playful antics could just tease her into joining him, as he is sometimes too naughty for her to resist. For the Gemini man, all that sexual intensity is a little suffocating; he needs to be able to breathe and see what's going on. At best they'll make a habit of replaying that first encounter, which is a highly engaging prospect. At worst, she'll be thinking about how soon she can begin faking an orgasm and getting the guy to fly away home.

SCORPIO WOMAN WITH **CANCER MAN**

In love: A love supreme! There's obviously a very natural flow of energy between these two when they first meet and whenever they get together thereafter. The Cancer man will win the Scorpio lady over completely with his gentle, loving ways and will totally adore her. She knows it, and although the Scorpio lady finds it very difficult to entrust her heart to someone, she'll finally have met the soul with whom it's possible. He'll never tread on her feelings and will care for her and protect her from anything that could possibly trouble her. She'll be happy to accept him together with all the depth of feeling he possesses, which he hides from the rest of the world. However, her need to really get to the bottom of him will, because of his constantly shifting emotions, be a labor of love that could last her a lifetime. He sees his Scorpio lady's love as a precious gift and will treat it that way, and although his moods can go up and down like a yo-yo and can become a little irritating, her unwavering strength will see her through. However, the Scorpio woman's tendency to lash out when she's feeling vulnerable could hurt the Cancer man more than she'll ever know. That's the worst-case scenario, but all in all, there's so much harmony in this relationship that the very few, minor irritations in it can easily be overcome. These two simply intoxicate one another with their compulsive, addictive love. This is one very happy union.

In bed: This man's the Scorpio lady's perfect prey. She won't just see him coming, she'll feel his vibe from way off, almost as though she's expecting him. But while she uses her special arts of seduction, his tough outer shell will give nothing away. He'll probably just sit there motionless, like a Crab, even though he's churning with lascivious desire. He wants her badly but somehow knows that if he gives in too soon, she'll lose interest. She likes a challenge, and he's happy to present her with one, then, just as her desire to have him reaches fever pitch, he'll surrender with a sweet eroticism and make love to her until she's left completely breathless. These two know exactly how to get to one other's sexual core. Her intense sexual passion is palpable but it's so deeply rooted in her emotional connection with her partner that it takes an equally emotionally tuned-in lover to satisfy her. Unless they're those rare demonstrative types who can't keep their hands off each other, the subtlety they display in front of other people completely belies what's really going on between these two. They share a deep yet very playful eroticism and they're so sweet with each other. This pair are made for each other—they fit together like spoons.

SCORPIO WOMAN WITH LEO MAN

In love: Put a Scorpio woman and a Leo man together and the stage is set for the seduction of the century. It will be high drama indeed! But which of them will be the seducer? It's a role they both enjoy and perform with enormous passion. This is a full-on relationship;

these two make a connection physically, mentally, and emotionally, though sometimes it's a combative connection. There is a sense of urgency in their relationship, but they both know that they need to proceed with caution. Each is aware of, and attracted to, the other's strength of character; however, both have very fixed ideas about how the relationship should work and they won't always be in agreement. When they're not, their passions could turn destructive. The Scorpio woman keeps her immense emotional energy under tight control, releasing it only when she feels safe in the intimacy of love. Her Leo man, however, needs her open adoration. He resents it when he feels her love is being handed to him piecemeal, as if to test his commitment, particularly since, in his heart, he's truly loyal and trustworthy. His flashy displays of affection and his extravagant love tokens are appealing up to a point but, without a dependable flow of emotional accord running between them, the Scorpio woman could suspect them of being little more than bribes to keep her quiet. The bond between them has the chance of being either powerful or painful.

 In bed: The Leo man can turn up a Scorpio woman's heat like no other! He'll offer her a cross between pleasure and pain on all levels—spiritual, emotional, and maybe even physical. And with her record-breaking levels of endurance, she'll drive him crazy with desire! There's a powerful passion between them that both will long to explore, so they'll spend plenty of nights enjoying hot, raunchy sex. This is one area of their relationship that's sure to be fulfilling. He needs to be adored and she can give him that on a sensual level, but she might draw the line at demeaning herself in outright worship. The need for each of them to be the controlling partner in this union could mean it ends up in a power struggle, but the fireworks that result will be explosive and exciting. The Scorpio woman needs to feel intimacy and intensity, as does the Leo man, but not every Leo man (despite his ardent nature) will find it easy to keep his fire burning when she pulls him into her deep wells of emotion. He may find her hunger for that kind of connection smothering and all-devouring, just as she, despite her sensual and erotic nature, may occasionally suspect his animalistic physicality of being egotistical, self-serving, and insensitive. With such a level of volatile energy between them, anything could happen in the bed they share; they should be careful not to burn each other out. It may be up to her to use her superb ability to set the pace.

SCORPIO WOMAN WITH VIRGO MAN

In love: The Scorpio woman is instinctive and, from the very beginning, she'll have recognized that there's much more to the Virgo man than is apparent on the surface. She likes depth, and he has it. Being with him is like having a therapy session; all sorts of buried urges start revealing themselves. He can't help himself when faced with her intense, penetrating mind; she frightens and fascinates him in equal measure. It's very thrilling. She'll love the way he responds to her on all levels and knows that she can get under his aloof exterior better than anyone. There's a very obvious sense of compatibility between these two, no matter in what circumstances they find themselves. In fact, they could become rather obsessive about each other to the exclusion of all else. When it comes to the long term, he's very good at organizing the practical, day-to-day necessities, which leaves her free to take care of the little things that add spice to the relationship—the Scorpio lady has a bottomless reserve of spicy ideas. The only downside is that, though he's pretty adaptable, he'll resent any efforts by her to control or manipulate him. If she tries, that could make him want to create some distance between them, which he'll do by revealing that slightly over-critical side of his nature. And if she perceives that he might be censuring her, then the Virgo man will soon feel that penetrating sting in the Scorpion tail, and boy, will it hurt!

 In bed: The Scorpio woman is just the one to unlock the Virgo man's deeply sexual tendencies. Is he Virgo the Virgin? Definitely not. He's hot—white hot, but he needs a woman like a Scorpio to set him alight. She won't believe what this man is capable of arousing in her when they get locked in the bedroom. She'll feel pure, unadulterated passion that keeps on burning until she can't stand it any more; she just won't know what's gotten into her! The Scorpio woman simply wells up with erotic energy at his slightest touch, while the Virgo man has skills that could surprise even the Scorpio lady. This is one time when he doesn't mind getting dirty, especially when it comes to talking, but he's also open to other suggestions simply because he finds her such a turn-on. She could persuade him to try anything, at least once. When it comes to the physical expression of their feelings, these two are in perfect accord. He'll be truly awash with loving feelings induced by her powerful yet embracing emotions, just as she will be touched by the way he conveys his gentle but strong need for her.

SCORPIO WOMAN WITH **LIBRA MAN**

 In love: Thanks to their mutual desire to connect with people on a personal level, the Libra man and Scorpio woman share some of the same feelings and views on life. Both know all the good things that there are about being in a relationship and they often also have a strong spiritual attraction. Her search for psychological understanding means that she appreciates his need to analyze their love life and get a more thorough knowledge of what makes it and her tick. His charm, backed up by brains, appeals to her penetrating mind and powerful femininity and she likes the impact that her attributes have on him. He really wants to be her guy, the one she turns to for everything, but her intuition tells her that he'll resist any intense, emotional expressions of feelings. He, meanwhile, finds it very difficult to convey what he feels in any way other than verbally. In short, he won't like her dragging out of him all the unpleasant things that he prefers to keep hidden. His light, flirty sociability can sometimes appear a little shallow to the Scorpio woman. For a while at least, this relationship can be a great voyage of discovery for the two of them, but for a more permanent arrangement, compromise is the key.

In bed: At times the Libra man will be everything a Scorpio woman could hope for in a lover. He's thoughtful, charming, and romantic, and he'll thoroughly enjoy setting the scene for their moments of sweet passion. His elegant seduction techniques will be great for building her anticipation. Candlelight, violins, bouquets of roses, and perfect sweet nothings whispered in her ear will have her in the mood for lovemaking more often than she'd be willing to admit. He's also open to her suggestions, although he's so considerate and so enjoys making her feel good that she'd be hard-pressed to find ways for him to improve. The Scorpio lady's sexiness inspires commitment to the pleasures of the flesh. To begin with, it's her powerful sensuality that attracts him, but after his first experience of sliding between the sheets with her, he'll just want to keep coming back for more. She's so sexually intuitive that she's able to control their connection, while he goes deeper and more compellingly into things, and that can unleash a storm of feelings. This is dangerous territory for him; he finds it highly exciting but, in the end, he just might not be able to match and sustain such deep levels of eroticism. They have slightly different styles, but if this Libra man takes his time in exploring those deep levels and brings along with him his sincere love for his Scorpio lady, then the magic of their sexual chemistry will do its thing and, given time, their lovemaking will get more and more amazing for them both.

SCORPIO WOMAN WITH **SCORPIO MAN**

 In love: When the Scorpio man and woman meet, there's such an incredibly powerful vibe between them that they'll both sense that they have something very special in common. It's when they realize that they're both Scorpios that the understanding really begins, and then things get beguiling. Never before have they experienced such an incredible feeling! The intensity of this relationship is so compelling that neither of them can resist it. When they fall in love, it's so deeply that the two of them can get lost in it and, even at the beginning, when they're both testing the water and cautiously feeling through the undercurrents for signs of danger, they get pulled under by their desire to discover more. When two Scorpios get together the rest of the world disappears. There's simply no room for anything in their lives but each other and exploring one another in every possible way. These two are a power couple who don't give a hoot for the romantic conventions of the outside world and who have their own code to live by. The relationship isn't without its problems, however; two people who are so committed to uncovering each other's secrets and vulnerabilities will both know exactly how to inflict a stinging attack on the other if their partner causes them to suffer any real, or even imagined, hurt. Despite that, they'll share some painfully tender moments. These two can thrive on the highs and lows of their relationship.

In bed: Black satin sheets, sweaty bodies, and skin that sizzles to the touch. Everything and anything can happen when two sexy, sensual Scorpios get down and dirty. Both enjoy the predatory power play that sex can offer, so games of domination and surrender may well set their pulses racing. Their bedside cabinets will hold their share of black leather, tassels, and studs, but it doesn't necessarily mean that that's all these two are into. They immerse themselves in the passion of lovemaking, and even for two people who like to be in control, there's a point at which they'll completely let go of themselves and reach nirvana. If they have time for anything else in their lives, it will be a miracle! They'll be totally engrossed in exploring each other's bodies, locking themselves away from the big wide world for days with the answering machine on and the curtains closed. Theirs will be a two-member club that meets in the Love Shack, and here, in attempting to penetrate to the very heart and soul of each other, they'll find themselves in a "no pain, no gain" situation. But never mind; they'll laugh in the face of danger and goad each other on to still more intense eroticism.

SCORPiO WOMAN WiTH **SAGiTTARiUS MAN**

In love: The Scorpio woman will be charmed and inspired by the adventurous soul of the Sagittarius man, just as he'll be intrigued and seduced by her controlled intensity. He'll make her laugh at the absurdity of life and will open her mind to new experiences and ideas that will provide her with plenty of mysteries—then he'll beg her to solve them. She'll fascinate him with the depth of her understanding, her way of exploring philosophical ideas from a psychological perspective, and her veiled feminine eroticism that will excite his own sense of masculinity. The attraction between these two is strong and it promises not only to be interesting and entertaining, but mind-expanding as well. However, it's a promise that's hard to keep because he can be elusive and she can be possessive, and somehow the two just can't be in a relationship together without him agreeing to have his freedom curtailed or her exercising tighter control on her jealousy. They have such an ardent two-way fascination with each other, however, that it would be difficult for them not to fall in love. They'll explore the deep, dark recesses of each other's fathomless souls and will gradually learn to trust one another, but it may take time, and perhaps more time than either might be willing to give. In the end, the relationship will be worth it if they both recognize the way that their egos keep them apart, and that it's their hearts that matter most. If they follow their hearts, then they'll go all the way.

In bed: The sex life of a Scorpio woman and a Sagittarius man is bound to be steamy! There's such a sexual pressure that builds up when they're together and things can get so intense between them that afterward they'll be picking pieces of each other off the walls, ceiling, and floor. This lusty man enjoys romping with her in bed or in any other place where they happen to be when he's aroused—and she will arouse him! He finds her very sexy indeed; it's almost as if she were weaving a kind of magic spell over him. She has a way of taking him deep inside his wild, animalistic nature; he gets so intoxicated with sensual delight that he behaves like a savage on the rampage—exactly what the Scorpio woman desires. He's adventurous and she's amazingly sensual, so together they'll go along dark alleys, through deep tunnels, then rocket up to the stratosphere. Things might get a little uncomfortable at times, but any place is worth a try! The possibilities are endless so they'll never get bored, even after years of being together. But there's one habit that the Sagittarius man has that the Scorpio lady will have to get used to if she wants to keep the peace: she shouldn't expect him to be there in the morning when she wakes up. He has places to go and people to see.

SCORPiO WOMAN WiTH **CAPRiCORN MAN**

 In love: A Scorpio woman will simply adore the emotional complexity of the Capricorn man. He's like an endless puzzle that she can explore, and because he's built his character on such firm foundations, she'll feel safe and secure in the expression of his love. He's the solid earth that can contain her watery depth of emotion. These two are good for one another; in many ways they're made for each other and they have a naturally strong affinity for one another. Both possess a kind of profound wisdom that each understands and needs in a partner, and they also share a dark sense of humor that brings out their wicked side. He aspires to great things and she could be the woman who helps him to achieve them, or even vice versa. There's a touch of the tormented soul about this man, but he never feels sorry for himself and that simply makes her love him even more. He, on the other hand, will treasure her femininity, strength, and commitment. He has no problem with her need to delve into the darker aspects of her own psyche and his. Indeed, he encourages her because he, too, longs for the creative outlet that her intensity, deep emotions, and eroticism bring to their relationship. If a few aspects of his character are destroyed in the process then, as far as he's concerned, they weren't worth having in the first place. These two are able to make sacrifices for one another without either demanding that they do, and both are equally willing to make this partnership last.

 In bed: This is sexual heaven for the Scorpio lady; her Capricorn man is earthy, horny, and totally addicted to his sensual pleasures. She'll never have to question his love; she really turns him on and he can't help but make it obvious to her every day and in a very physical way. Whether it's the first embrace of the morning or the last little hug at night, she'll know it alright. There's always a subtle erotic hint present in her aura and it simply seems to envelop them both when they're together, raising their sexual awareness imperceptibly, but always leaving them ready and willing to get it on in an instant. Her predatory, penetrating gaze seduces him completely and he simply can't wait to return the compliment. It delights the Scorpio woman that he's so insatiably hungry for all the delicious sexual delicacies she has to offer. One touch leads to a stroke, which leads to a caress, and that takes them all the way down that slippery slope again and again. He could be the only man who has what it takes to absorb the entire ocean of her passions, or at least it seems that way. She could throw the whole weight of her intense eroticism, as well as her body, against him and he'd emerge breathless but eager for more.

SCORPIO WOMAN WITH **AQUARIUS MAN**

In love: The Scorpio woman finds a hell of a lot to like about the Aquarius man. He's a loyal, inventive, and intelligent bright spark, and she likes his energy. She may even fall in love with him because she finds his dynamism hard to resist. He seems to have all the qualities that she admires and requires from a lover. She'll be intrigued by his aloof, eccentric behavior, thinking that it's a cover for vast emotional reserves like her own; however, while they may be vast, they have very little to do with emotion. He operates in a realm of pure thought and mental complexity but she's certainly clever enough to draw him into the sort of exciting, exploratory conversations that he enjoys. Her take on things comes from a thoroughly different but interesting perspective and he respects her for it. He'll probably even love her for it, but he could resent her propensity to try to tempt a deeper emotional response from him. He simply doesn't do "irrational." When they're out on the town, the two of them make a fabulous team, but it's probably more as friends than lovers. Although the Scorpio lady prefers emotional depth, the fact that they can be friends is something worth having. If she's willing to let go of herself enough to be with him, he'll love her for it. These two won't let each other down in the loyalty stakes and will always find something to discuss. Once they're attached, it would be difficult and undesirable to detach them.

 In bed: Strange sex! There's no other way to describe the Scorpio woman and Aquarius man's sensual coupling. If strange sex appeals to them both, and chances are that it will, then their bedroom experience could go on for longer than anyone expects, least of all themselves! The Aquarius man is just a little bit different from any other lover that the Scorpio lady has ever had. He can be so inventive that he makes the *Kama Sutra* look like a boring "how-to" manual. But he might not have it in him to get this woman's juices really flowing because his package doesn't come with the emotional investment she needs. She doesn't simply want technical know-how and clever tricks that are designed to bring her to orgasm; she must have intense, deep, searing passion. But she'll certainly want to get it on with him because he has an intriguing allure and she's into losing herself in a variety of ways. But once may be enough. He'll be excited by her eroticism but may very well drown in her sea of emotional sensuality, for the Aquarius man can only do emotions in a mechanical kind of way and will back off when he finds it too difficult to keep up. For an Air type like him, not being able to breathe or think his way through an experience means that he's unable to access his mental fantasies, and that's where he finds the most potent sexual satisfaction.

SCORPIO WOMAN WITH **PISCES MAN**

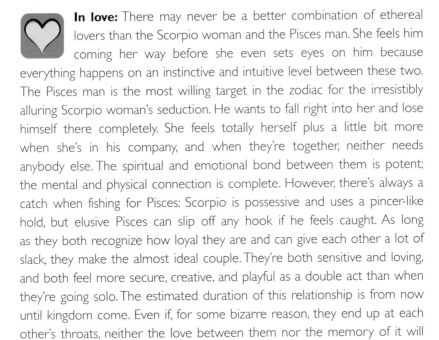 **In love:** There may never be a better combination of ethereal lovers than the Scorpio woman and the Pisces man. She feels him coming her way before she even sets eyes on him because everything happens on an instinctive and intuitive level between these two. The Pisces man is the most willing target in the zodiac for the irresistibly alluring Scorpio woman's seduction. He wants to fall right into her and lose himself there completely. She feels totally herself plus a little bit more when she's in his company, and when they're together, neither needs anybody else. The spiritual and emotional bond between them is potent; the mental and physical connection is complete. However, there's always a catch when fishing for Pisces: Scorpio is possessive and uses a pincer-like hold, but elusive Pisces can slip off any hook if he feels caught. As long as they both recognize how loyal they are and can give each other a lot of slack, they make the almost ideal couple. They're both sensitive and loving, and both feel more secure, creative, and playful as a double act than when they're going solo. The estimated duration of this relationship is from now until kingdom come. Even if, for some bizarre reason, they end up at each other's throats, neither the love between them nor the memory of it will ever die. There's an element of destiny about their being together, so if this magical couple don't manage to work it out in this lifetime, they'll do so the next time around.

In bed: In a word—intoxicating! Getting dreamily drunk on love and addicted to the effects of this highly emotional coupling is only to be expected. If they're looking for an out-of-body experience, then the Scorpio woman will find sex with a Pisces man is about the closest thing to it, and vice versa. When these two Water signs get down to it, they go deep, deep down. There are no limits to the depths of their closeness or to the heights to which their spirits soar when the passionate Scorpio woman meets up with the ultimately romantic Pisces man. This is mutual worship at its very best. He'll sacrifice himself to her sexual pleasure but will gain the world in return, and she'll keep for him exclusively the erotic intensity of her sweet, sensitive heart. It will be as though she were wearing an invisible chastity belt that only his love key can open. These two are inclined to lose all concept of time and space when they're together; even a short moment of afternoon delight could end up in a seriously expanded time warp. On occasions like that it would be wise to check the calendar rather than the clock.

THE SCORPIO MAN IN LOVE

Charismatic, enigmatic, and sexually savvy, the Scorpio man is hard to resist but he's not what he appears to be on the surface. Underneath that serenely dignified and controlled exterior lies an inferno of passion. He seems to possess something that all women want, yet are perhaps a little frightened of having. He's also intuitive and compelling, so firstly, he won't need a women to strip off to know what her body looks like underneath and, secondly, he'll let her know just when she's allowed to remove each item of her clothing!

The Scorpio man gives all his brooding, passionate, sensual intensity to his beloved, and he expects no less in return. This man is looking for a relationship with a special lady that offers him a deep connection, a mystical experience, a transcendental coupling, and if these are present, he'll find them via eroticism and sexuality. Because this deep inner bond is so important to him, he can display possessive, jealous tendencies if his lady ever dares to stray, or worse, if someone tries to come between them. Any such person will be treated to the sort of firework display and volatile emotional outbursts that this sign is so famous for.

Scorpio man is a pillar of strength to his lady in times of need, but he also likes his lady to show a bit of strength as well. He'll only respect her if she's his match, but he's not looking for a match in physical, intellectual, emotional, or even spiritual terms; it's more about the woman as a whole. This might sound a little calculating but he feels as though his self-worth is reflected in her, and since he's very much into power and presence, she'll need to be able to keep her side up as much as he does.

Scorpios hate secrets, unless of course the secrets are their own, so Scorpio man is fiercely protective of his privacy, and if his woman tries to pry too far too soon, she'll get short shrift. He'll open up a little at a time and in his own time. But it's worth making an effort to keep this man because he has so much to offer in terms of security, both material and emotional. He is torrentially tempestuous, however, which not every woman can handle. He's not afraid of saying what he feels, but he's not into mindless insults, so what he does have to say when he's heated is likely to be straight and to the point; there won't be any sugarcoating. And because he's a sensitive man who understands human nature, he can cope with other people's outbursts. He's not quick to forgive, though, and can be vindictive, but as long as everyone plays fair, there won't be a problem. The fact is that his heart can be as soft as anyone else's but it takes him time to trust and truly hand that heart over; but when he does, he does so completely. Chances are that he's been hurt in the past, which is why he can play so hard to get, but he is capable of feeling all the pain and joy of love, and once smitten, he won't let go. A strong, sexy, faithful woman is exactly what he needs.

SCORPIO MAN WITH **ARIES WOMAN**

 In love: There's a powerful magnetic attraction between these two, a challenge that neither will be able to ignore very easily. Both signs are ruled by Mars, so the Scorpio man and the Aries woman will naturally have a shared sympathy for one another. He's all self-confidence and controlled, hidden passion, while she's all self-confidence and overt, unbridled passion. Passion is what they have in common, not just the lusty kind, but the kind that generates action and energy. The fuel that they create between them would certainly fire a rocket into space and beyond. They're a powerful pair and can easily perceive one another's fighting spirit and admire it—that is, until they're fighting with each other, which is something that can happen quite easily if these two aren't careful. Careful? An Aries woman? She can be terribly thoughtless at times, which will cut her surprisingly sensitive Scorpio man to the quick. Then heaven help her. He will be sure to let her know with stinging accuracy just how dreadfully she has behaved, and it will all escalate from there. They are both competitive but in different ways. She's the obvious up-front one, while he's discreet and devious. Most Aries girls can bounce back from anything, but she'll know never to make the same mistake twice when she's involved with a Scorpio man. If he truly wants to keep her, he'll need to adjust his tolerance levels to accommodate this wild woman's tactics, but much to his frustration, he'll never really possess her.

In bed: He'll think he's got her wrapped around his finger but she's far too independent to be tied down in such a restraining manner. This sexual relationship is tempestuous at best and volatile at worst. The Scorpio man has the capacity to completely enslave the Aries woman in the bedroom, and he won't give her time to think about anything other than indulging in their passionate pursuits. He is delighted not only that she can match him in physical intensity, but also that her appetite for sex is as keen as his own. Certainly, their neighbors will be aware of their carnal capers, but this won't bother either of them. They will be so into each other that nothing else matters. Scorpio is known as a manipulative sign, so she should watch how he plays her — all over. There's no doubt this is an intense and compelling union. As though she were on a mission, the Aries woman knows what she wants when it comes to sex, and so does the Scorpio man. Together they make an awesome duo that most couples can only dream of. They could end up either making love for the world or fighting to the bitter end. What this couple needs is less armor and more *amour*.

SCORPIO MAN WITH **TAURUS WOMAN**

In love: Being an Earth sign, the Taurus woman will certainly enjoy having the Scorpio man as her excavation project. He's very deep and seemingly dark, but her senses inform her that it would be worth the effort of getting to the bottom of him. Once he gets used to her no-nonsense way of handling him, he'll not only be intrigued, he'll be hooked! He likes the way that she knows her own mind, is quietly in control of herself, and doesn't get flustered when he tries to probe her sensitive spots. This is one woman that the Scorpio man will not be able to play like a yo-yo. She won't even notice it if he attempts to manipulate her. She doesn't operate that way and never expects anyone else to, so it just passes over her like a wave on the seashore. The Scorpio man is after a deep and lasting intimacy and he needs a woman who will give herself to him fully, but until then he's happy to play around, so he may try to test her commitment during the formative stages of their relationship. But the Taurus woman is very matter-of-fact and, as a Bull, she certainly won't take any nonsense. The end-result will be that they'll never let each other down because they truly respect one another. Scorpio is ruled by Mars and Taurus by Venus—the cosmic lovers. That, plus the fact that the signs are opposite one another in the zodiac, means that there is an affinity binding them together like magnets. He is as hypnotic as she is alluring. Together they're a truly potent mixture.

 In bed: The Taurus woman, being so deliciously indulgent and highly sensual, is a wonderfully rich lover. This suits the Scorpio man just fine, as he is intense, brooding, and always horny. He's perfect at handling her vast resources of sexual energy. This is one sizzling combination, and there is serious Tantric potential here! Patient as the Taurus woman is, however, when she gets it on with her Scorpio man, that patience flies right out of the window. Both are intensely passionate, but there's also mutual trust between them, which is just as well because their jealous rages are as intense as their sexual attractiveness. And since both are very aware of the destructive potential in their powerful emotions, it's unlikely they'll create any real trouble for each other with other partners, although it wouldn't be beyond the Scorpio man to try to spice up a party and arouse his Taurus lady's possessiveness with a hint of flirting. Once they get home to bed, though, they'll be as keen and eager as each other—but he won't want to let her know this too soon! He's a lover who's into teasing and titillating and he will be totally immersed in bringing her right to the edge. Luckily he doesn't believe in half-measures. He'll take her all the way.

SCORPIO MAN WITH GEMINI WOMAN

In love: At first, the Scorpio man might be tempted to write off the Gemini woman as a delicate, amusing, but rather shallow female. And he'd be worried—and with good reason—that he might not be able to hold her attention long enough to form the intimate bond that he craves. She may be blind to his more attractive qualities, since any attempts at flirting with him only encourage his penetrating inspection, and this sends her flitting nervously away before she can really get to know him. If she treats him as a fleeting curiosity then she'll find that it's his attention that wanders first, which is something this girl is just not used to. He will, of course, want the physicality that she can offer and will even be attracted by the energetic way she moves about the room. He also has the gall to believe that he knows her every thought, but, in fact, this isn't so far from the truth. Meanwhile, the Gemini woman might find the Scorpio man a little scary at first, with his intense way of looking at her and his brooding manner. She'll feel as if he's going to eat her up, and he might do if she's lucky! If she takes her time and can settle her nerves while this predatory man is putting her under the microscope, she'll find him as compelling as an erotic novel. If he knows what's good for him, he'll mind his manners and allow this love to grow. It might just stand the test of time and mature rather nicely.

 In bed: When it comes to sex, the last thing this guy wants is a bit of lighthearted slap and tickle. For him, achieving deep and meaningful satisfaction is absolutely crucial. He doesn't mind the adjustment period that she'll need in order to adapt to his zealous sexual style. This phase can provoke some passionate gestures from him and some strong statements from her about limits. To him there's nothing like feelings being aired to fire up his already brooding libido, but this won't necessarily be a turn-on for her. However, at the mere thought of having her, he can turn into a keen, mean, loving machine in a matter of seconds, and that's difficult for any woman to resist. He'll happily indulge her desires by involving himself fully in playing with her collection of erotic toys, but should she ever seem to prefer them to him, then his sexual jealousy knows no bounds. If he ever suspects that she is about to change her mind about him, that's sure to put him in a gloomy mood. And Scorpio never forgives or forgets. But she'll have turned him on as never before!

SCORPIO MAN WITH **CANCER WOMAN**

 In love: No matter what he says, or how well he hides it, the Scorpio man is fiercely possessive, which is why the Cancer woman's innate need for protection will appeal to him so much. Her intuition tells her that there is something very special lying deep in the heart of this man, an emotional power that touches her instinctively. She feels his raw passion, and accepts his need to keep it under tight control, but she'd really like nothing better than to have him offer it to her to treasure and cherish. These two may take their time, testing out the potential in their relationship before they are willing to jump in at the deep end. Once they do take the plunge, however, they do so with a shared sense of commitment and then they can begin to discover just how creative and personally expansive their relationship can be. The Scorpio man gives off strong sexual vibes to all females but he won't let his Cancer woman down because, once she's his, he'll remain totally loyal. She shouldn't try to understand him but just accept him together with all his awesome potency. The female crab has a profound capacity for intuitively comprehending this man and when she's with him that will give her the peace of mind she needs. Their closeness is a closeness of the heart, a place where words are unnecessary. The Scorpio man won't want to let this lovely lady go once he gets a taste for her, for he knows that he'll probably never meet another woman like her.

In bed: Cancer and Scorpio, two Water signs, will have a whale of a time in bed! These two lovers so enjoy being together that even if someone threw them a life preserver, they wouldn't come up to grab it. Who needs air when they can keep on swallowing each other's hot and horny breath! The Scorpio man is so sexually intuitive that even if the Cancer woman put a blindfold on him for an added thrill, he would easily find her pleasure zones. Yes, this couple will most certainly get it on. She may not be able to surprise him, but he'll always be up for her. Any attempt to seduce him may look bungled; instead, all she really has to do is keep up her little sideways dance and be ready with open arms, eyes, and attitude! When these two get into bed together, a tidal wave of passion washes over them and sends them spinning in ecstasy. There's definitely a dangerous quality to his eroticism, which may make her wary but the Scorpio man knows how to coax the Cancer lady out of her shell.

SCORPIO MAN WITH **LEO WOMAN**

In love: He's magnetic: people—particularly women—are drawn to him. The Leo woman may not know why she wants him, but there's something compelling about the Scorpio man and she has to find out more. This is a tempestuous affair, full of love and hate, but no indifference. It's likely that he can show her a thing or two about another side of loving—a bed of roses will always have the occasional thorn. This isn't the kind of relationship that will survive on love alone for, although the Leo woman and the Scorpio man can be loving, kind, and generous toward each other, they can also be angry and spiteful. However, if these two have other interests in common that are anything but common—for example, an amazing physical relationship—their connection will be sealed by fate. Fate is double-edged and as they can both be rather sharp, they could end up with a fatal attraction for each other that they have difficulty both holding onto and letting go. No one will fill them with more than each other so they could easily become addicted to the thrill of their fierce, shared passion. It's a tough one to call, because when they're good together, they're very, very good, but when they're bad, it's horrid.

 In bed: If the Scorpio man comes on to the Leo lady first, he probably won't stand a chance; she'll simply flick her tail at him and saunter off without a backward glance. But if he sits back and plays hard to get, she won't like being ignored and may just go out of her way to seduce him. It'll be well worth her while because he's no amateur. His lovemaking will hit her like a tidal wave and he can get very naughty, but the Leo woman already has her own ideas about what she'd like in bed. He knows this but, just to build some tension, he might resist. With her passions being held under such tight control, she'll quickly get fed up with playing the game and will force him into doing things her way—and immediately! She may not even realize that she's been deliberately manipulated into just this kind of performance, but if she does, then never mind; she'll put on a show anyway. They say all's fair in love and war, but with these two on it, any bed will definitely look like a field of battle—and neither will make any apologies for the battle scars. This pairing could either end up as one hot and steamy affair or simply as two people who are mad at one another.

SCORPIO MAN WITH VIRGO WOMAN

In love: It really appeals to the Virgo woman's fantasy to be the maiden on whom the predatory Scorpio has set his sights, and this guy won't let her down on that score. He truly exudes a dangerous intensity when he's in seduction mode. Their courtship dance feels totally instinctive; whatever her age, she'll play the demure young woman who's unaware of the imminent threat to her innocence, yet she's just waiting for him. He'll play the dark prince who comes along and snatches her away from her virtuous existence. Although both are very self-contained during early courtship, that just raises their expectations for a truly deep involvement, but it makes the Virgo lady a little nervous because part of her wants to remain detached from such an all-consuming passion. She knows it will be hard to keep her purity intact once he starts delving into her heart and soul, and yet she is thrilled at the reaction she gets simply from being in his company. He instinctively senses her passionate side, which she keeps so well hidden; the idea of unlocking it will drive him crazy with desire! These two could easily get caught up revolving around each other, getting deeper into each other's psyches to the exclusion of all else. It's a delicious feeling; should they ever part, they'll always be marked with the profound love that they once shared.

In bed: He's a really sexy beast! The Scorpio man seems to know just what to do to turn the Virgo woman into a quivering wench, wanton with desire. Her thoughts will naturally turn to eroticism wherever she is if there's a Scorpio lover by her side, and he'll be insatiable in his desire for her. These two seem to walk around in a world of their own, totally absorbed in each other's delectable sexiness. But they really should keep an eye out for those closed-circuit TV cameras! On the other hand, perhaps the cameras will add to the excitement! Another dimension to this partnership's sensual connection is that they both have inquiring minds, which means that they won't balk at exploring areas of their sexuality that others would be inclined to leave alone. They are, however, both sensitive enough to make sure that the other is completely comfortable with any experimentation. This very exclusive, private behavior between the two of them helps them to forge a truly deep and trusting bond.

SCORPIO MAN WITH **LIBRA WOMAN**

 In love: The Scorpio man loves a challenge and he knows just how he's going to get his Libra woman—or so he thinks. He'll go after her single-mindedly, using some of the most thrilling seduction techniques that she's ever encountered, but she's pretty savvy when it comes to one-on-one tricks and will be completely clued in on what he's up to. She certainly likes it, but is perhaps not so sure that she wants it. Maybe at first she just enjoys playing hard to get, or maybe she senses that she could be going down a seriously dangerous route with this guy, because his version of one-on-one tricks is a bit more grown-up than her own. He knows what he wants and likes what he sees on the surface. He'll assume that there's a lot more to uncover, but he might not get what he expects! The question she'll keep asking herself is, does she have what it takes to keep him interested? The answer is, probably, but what she should be asking is, does she want to keep him interested? Scorpio man can be very manipulative and there's a chance that the Libra lady might not like the way he wants to mold her. There's an undeniable attraction between these two but they also have a few sticking points to get over first. As long as they get stuck on each other and don't get stuck on those points, then this is a mutually fascinating love affair that could last and last.

 In bed: The Scorpio man loves to get right up close and personal and when it comes to sex, that's his mission statement. He'll manipulate his way right to his Libra lady's most sensitive spots. He's also a man who likes to be on top, and in more ways than one! He may try a variety of techniques in order to elicit some reaction from her, but though she's the mistress of reactions, he might not quite understand how that necessitates her giving a running commentary on the experience and verbalizing all the sexy thoughts that are running through her head. If he allows Lady Libra to take the lead, the dark and dangerous Scorpio man might find her bright and breezy approach to lovemaking a little too light for his tastes, although he always finds playing the villain to her damsel in distress quite a turn-on. His sexual appetites run deeper than she may be prepared to go, for her natural tendency is to soar beyond any purely physical sensuality. If she gives him a chance, then he could seduce her around to his way of thinking. He's hot, tasty, and truly masterful at creating erotic tension, so it would be hard for the Libra lady not to succumb to his advances. Then she'll melt in his embrace and know that she's in for a really rocking time.

SCORPIO MAN WITH **SCORPIO WOMAN**

See pages 66–67.

SCORPIO MAN WITH **SAGITTARIUS WOMAN**

In love: When the Scorpio man focuses his laser-like intensity on the hard-to-get Sagittarius woman, he'll make her squirm in a most delicious way! She can sense danger and excitement and she's a sucker for a challenge. He, meanwhile, is fascinated by everything about the adventurous Sagittarius woman. This is a life puzzle that neither participant can wait to solve and both long to follow the titillating road of discovery that leads to each other. She is open and bold about it, while he is secretive and prone to reading too much into everything. However, they share a fascination with life and all its deeper and higher meanings, so their spiritual connection is likely to be very strong. The downside is that half the time, living with the Scorpio man will be like walking on eggshells because he's so sensitive; the spontaneous Sagittarius woman, who prefers to just get on with things, could find it all very draining. They're both on their own paths and going in different directions, so in time, their paths may no longer cross and the distance could get too great between them. The good news is that both are searching for a deeper, more thorough understanding of the world and when they compare notes, they'll find that the feeling's mutual. Most encouraging of all, of course, is the fact that they'll constantly present each other with the kind of challenge that just keeps them going on and on together. They'll always have something to say to and learn from one another, and that will keep this fire alive.

 In bed: Imagine the scene. The lusty Sagittarius woman meets the insatiable Scorpio man; Fire meets Water. Things get seriously hot and steamy until the sexual passions are boiling over! This sexual relationship is not for the fainthearted and neither of them is likely to feel the slightest hint of indifference. The Scorpio man's preference is to drag the Sagittarius woman back to his dark and dangerous den for some deeply erotic experiences, while she'll be dreaming about taking him by the hand to a mountaintop to make love under the stars until dawn. If he had his way, she'd probably end up handcuffed to the bedpost and if she had her way, they'd both be swinging from the treetops. They both want each other like mad, but they also both want the other to do it their way like mad. There are many features of their sex life that will make this affair an exotic, erotic heaven, but there's also one issue that will be more difficult to deal with, and that is that the Sagittarius woman will find it almost impossible to accept Scorpio's jealousy. For she needs her freedom and she just can't give him the security and total commitment that he needs. In the long term, the Scorpio man's demands could make it difficult to sustain great sex while the Sagittarius lady's absence will make sex nonexistent. Mutual trust, however, could help to keep the thrust of this relationship going.

SCORPIO MAN WITH **CAPRICORN WOMAN**

 In love: This is a fatal attraction but not at all like the movie of the same name—there's no bunny-boiling here! These two both feel a sense of mind-blowing potential when they're in each other's company, so in the early days they'll treat each other with reverence and respect—and that means that it would be difficult for them not to fall seriously in love. And it is, indeed, a very serious business for both of them for, wherever they are and whatever they're doing, the intensity of their feelings is only just beneath the surface. It consumes them both with a force that's almost scary in its power and will make them lose their heads when they lose their hearts, obliging them to behave in ways that are alien to them. They feel such an unbreakable bond and they give each other such strength that, as a couple, they're invincible. The Scorpio man follows his instincts and he'll sense that, with the Capricorn woman, there's the possibility of a long-lasting love affair, so he'll be on his best behavior. She, for her part, is always on her best behavior; all she'll want to do is devote herself to him. But all this intensity has the capacity to tear into both of them and hurt really deep down if they're not careful to keep a sense of humor and do unto the other as they would be done by. However, neither will be willing to give up easily on this relationship; it affects them both too deeply—emotionally, mentally, and physically.

 In bed: The Scorpio man is on fire with lust for the cool Capricorn lady, but something tells him that he has to contain himself until she gives him the green light. He's not used to waiting or being told what to do, but there's a certain quality about her that tells him she's worth waiting for, so he'd better be serious. Once she gives him the go-ahead, he'll hardly wait for another breath before he'll want to rip her clothes off, take her in his arms, and make love to her until she literally screams with pleasure! She's usually rather good at self-restraint so she may be a little surprised by her own reaction. This is a man who sneaks into erogenous zones that she didn't even know she had. He's a dangerous predator, but that won't stop her from wanting more. Her strong physical desires are more than a match for his passion. Together, the Scorpio man and Capricorn woman won't be able to go any deeper than this level of eroticism. This is something unique and totally exhilarating—sex and sensuality as they've never had it before. It rocks their world and sets a standard that most other lovers would find difficult to attain. It's nothing but pure, passionate pleasure taken to its extreme. When will they ever find the time to sleep?

SCORPIO MAN WITH **AQUARIUS WOMAN**

In love: Initially, the attraction between an Aquarius lady and a Scorpio man is strong; both like to get into people's heads and find out what makes them tick and once they discover a little more about one another, they'll be even more intrigued. But when the Aquarius lady comes up against all that dark, brooding intensity in the Scorpio man, she'll want to shy away, and in most cases that would be the right thing to do. But if she likes to live dangerously, then he's the man for her. Their deep understanding of the mysteries of life and their fascination with things spiritual give them some common ground on which to start building their love. At times, however, stubbornness on both sides could result in an impasse. To top that, he's very possessive and jealous, and that sort of thing simply makes Aquarius retreat. She's naturally independent and won't make it easy for the Scorpio man to weave those bonds of emotional intimacy that have to be firmly in place for him before he'll expose that side of his nature that she'd find so precious and endearing. She's unlikely to have the tolerance or emotional sensitivity to see anything other than the negative side of his romantic character. There's potential here, but with all the angst that develops from their differences, would either of them really want it to last forever? They'd have to be gluttons for punishment, and if they are, there would need to be another factor to seductively bind them together. And so to bed…

In bed: The Scorpio man's fierce passion is all very thrilling and sexy, but his emotions could be a little overpowering for the cool Aquarius woman. She rather likes the idea of this sexual relationship and delights in sharing her fantasies with him until he turns to steam and is carried ever upward by her sexy words. But the reality of totally merging with him at such a high level might not be so wonderful for her! This relationship could simply be too stormy, and although the electricity it generates is quite exhilarating, when the Scorpio man gathers himself into an ominous dark cloud, the threat of a driving rain of emotion makes the Aquarius woman shiver, and not perhaps in the way he'd hope! She's very attracted to pleasure and amusements, and he'll offer her just about the best ride in the fair—an eye-popping, breathtaking, white-knuckle ride that's so moving, she won't know whether to laugh or cry when it finally comes to a stop. There's also an element of competition between these two individuals so they could well fight for control, for instance, to see who gets the right to tie whom to the bedposts. This sort of tussle is lots of fun for a while, particularly for the Scorpio man, who likes to have a spirited lady in his bed, but in the long run, unless this particular Aquarius woman is willing to submit to him, she might feel that burning sting of his Scorpion's tail. And when that happens, it stops being amusing; the whole thing could simply get too dark and scary for her to deal with.

SCORPIO MAN WITH **PISCES WOMAN**

In love: The Scorpio man is passionately possessive and sexually jealous where the Pisces lady is concerned. If he could have his way, she'd be tied to the bed and strapped into a chastity belt when he's out. If he earns her trust, she'll do as he asks simply because he gives her what she really wants—good loving, great sex, and a sense of strength and security. He'll never find a woman who's more agreeable to his demands; in fact, she might seem a little too wet to some men, but not to the Scorpio man. He knows exactly what to do with her and brings out the best in her by handling her supersensitivity to perfection. It's true that he can be somewhat manipulative, but she's wise to it and will either choose to flow with it or, simply, around it. Her romanticism, far from being a shallow need for candlelit dinners and love tokens, opens up doors to a spiritual realm that he longs to explore. The Scorpio man wants to delve deeply into the Pisces lady and reach the parts that other men simply cannot reach. These two won't even need to talk about it to know that there's a huge dose of magic in the feelings that they evoke in one another. This partnership works very well; all the elements necessary for a merging of heart and soul are present. There may never be another relationship quite like this one for emotional intensity; neither will want to throw it away.

In bed: The Pisces lady has been dreaming about her knight in shining armor from a very young age. She's always known that one day she'd meet a man who could burst the dam of her fathomless sexuality. Well, here comes Mr. Scorpio. He's that man, so get ready to burst! Meanwhile, all he wants is a woman who's not frightened off by his powerful sex drive. And here she is! She's not really totally aware of what she's walking into but her naive trust allows her to experience fully the wonders of what the Scorpio man has to offer. Other women can leave him feeling like a cold mountain stream, but a sensual sex session with the Lady Fish turns him into a bubbling, steaming-hot geyser! Old Faithful will seem like nothing more than a dripping faucet compared to them. Mr. Scorpio's intensity moves her in deep places and she won't be able to drift away unless he gives her permission because his sexual prowess will keep on luring her back for more. Her erotic creativity will mystify him so much that he'll have to use all his penetrating powers of detection to solve the puzzle that she poses. There'll be many "Eureka!" moments along the way to them reaching their final conclusion. It's rare to find such mutually fulfilling sexual chemistry between two people; they could write the book of hot love. Although both Scorpio and Pisces are subtle signs, the dirty grins that they'll wear when they're with one another will say it all!